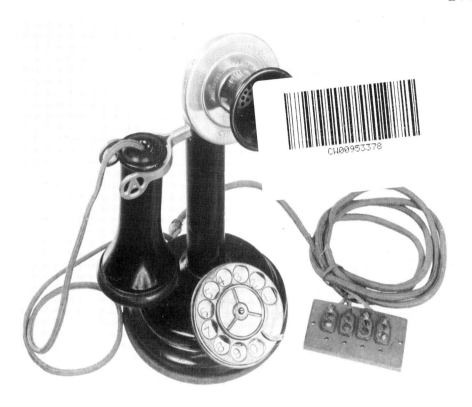

CW00953378

Britain's first dial telephone exchange opened in 1912 at Epsom in Surrey. The telephones used were standard American instruments, supplied by the Automatic Telephone Manufacturing Company of Liverpool. The dial is the number 1 type.

OLD TELEPHONES

Andrew Emmerson

Shire Publications Ltd

CONTENTS

Published in 2000 by Shire Publications Ltd, Cromwell House, Church Street, Princes Risborough, Buckinghamshire HP27 9AA, UK. Website: www.shirebooks.co.uk Copyright © 1986 by Andrew Emmerson. First published 1986; reprinted 1990, 1994 and 2000. Shire Album 161. ISBN 0 85263 781 0.

Printed in Great Britain by CIT Printing Services Ltd, Press Buildings, Merlins Bridge, Haverfordwest, Pembrokeshire SA61 1XF.

British Library Cataloguing in Publication Data: Emmerson, Andrew. Old telephones. — Shire Albums; v. 161) 1. Telephone — Great Britain — Equipment and supplies — History. I. Title 621. 385. TK 6057. ISBN 0-85263-781-0.

ACKNOWLEDGEMENTS

   The author is grateful to all those who helped in the production of this book and especially to Neil Johannessen, manager of the BT Museum, for his encouragement to bring this project to fruition. Illustrations are mainly from the BT Museum archives and are reproduced by their kind permission. The photographs on pages 12 (lower), 24, 25 and 28 (lower) are from the author's collection.

COVER: *One of the most attractive telephones ever designed, the skeleton type. This example is the British Post Office number 16 type and was used from about 1900 onwards.*

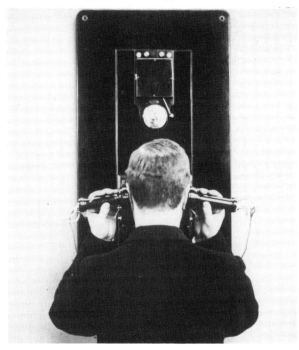

LEFT: *A photograph dated 1900 showing a wall telephone and the correct method of holding receivers.*

We cannot look at old telephones without a thought for the operators who connected the calls. This view of Woolwich exchange dates from 1927 but could have been taken thirty years earlier or later, so little did manual exchanges alter.

INTRODUCTION

A long time has passed since the invention of the telephone in 1876 and it is not surprising that the shape and form of the telephone instrument have changed over the years. It is more surprising that so little has changed technically: one of Bell's original instruments could be wired to a modern telephone and they could be made to work together.

This is not to deny the considerable technical improvements made to telephones and to telephone systems over the years, and this book sets out to describe those changes. It also describes the telephones in use during those times, because although the network is still with us most of the old telephones are not. For people who enjoy looking at old telephones for their own sake this book will need no further justification, and collectors may find it helpful for identifying items. It should also interest others who wish to put telephones in the broader context of their past and may encourage readers to spot more old telephones while watching films or visiting museums.

3

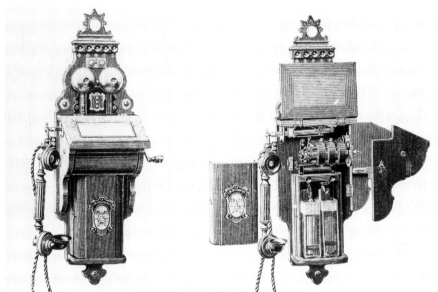

An Ericsson wall telephone from around 1900 and its mechanism. Note the magneto generator for calling the exchange and the Leclanché cells for powering the microphone.

HOW TELEPHONES WORK

Expressed very simply, the telephone is a device which converts sound waves into electrical currents, transmits them down a pair of wires to another place and then turns the currents back into sounds we can hear. Bound up in this is a system for connecting one person with another and letting that other person know there is someone who wishes to speak with him. The system is called the exchange network, though not all telephones are connected to exchanges: some are on private point-to-point systems and others are used for intercommunication systems in shops and offices.

The parts of the telephone which do the talking and listening are called the microphone (or transmitter) and the receiver. In many modern telephones both microphone and receiver are rather like miniature loudspeakers, consisting of a diaphragm and an electromagnet coil. Sound waves reaching the microphone cause the diaphragm to vibrate the coil and generate minute electric currents. An internal network amplifies this current and sends it down the two line wires to the exchange. Some of current is also

fed back to the caller's own receiver as 'sidetone' to avoid giving the effect of a totally dead instrument. The receiver does the opposite of the microphone: electric currents in the electromagnet attract and repel the diaphragm in the receiver or earpiece so as to convert the signals back to sound. These are the very basic principles; patterns of microphone and receiver have varied over the years, as have the methods of calling the other party to the conversation.

Many old telephones were fitted with hand generators or 'magnetos' which rang the distant bell direct (or caused an indicator to drop at the exchange). These telephones also needed their own power source (batteries) for the microphone and are known as 'local battery' or LB instruments; they are still used on some lines and as field telephones, etcetera.

Magneto generators were expensive to provide and the next development was to detect at the exchange when the subscriber lifted his or her handset to make a call. This system was called CBS (central battery signalling) and telephones still needed a battery to power the micro-

4

phone. A means was soon found of feeding voltage for the microphone down the line from the exchange: at last telephone customers could do away with the bulky and often messy batteries which had to be kept near the telephone. This system is known as CB (central battery) working.

All the telephone systems described so far have been manual ones, with operators taking the wanted number and connecting the calls. On LB exchanges, before lifting the receiver the caller also had to turn the handle of the generator smartly: this alerted the operator. At the end of each call subscribers had to indicate they had finished by turning the handle again — known as ringing off. The days of the manual systems were numbered, though, from 1889, when a Kansas City undertaker, Almon B. Strowger, had an idea. He suspected that calls for his business were being diverted to that of a rival, whose wife worked on the town's telephone exchange. Strowger set about devising a mechanism which connected calls mechanically and anonymously. The system, in which the customer uses a dial to indicate the number of the desired subscriber, is still in use today and also bears Strowger's name. There have been other mechanisms for connecting calls automatically, using relays, crossbar switches and computers, and the calling device is often now a keypad, but the principles of automatic telephony have not changed since 1889.

BUZZ, CLICK, RAT-A-TAT-TAT . . .

Buzzing, clicking, rat-a-tat-tat — tiny wheels turning, switches interlocking, impulses passed on — your robot telephone exchange at work — buzzing, clicking, rat-a-tat-tat . . . Ten thousand telephone numbers, ten million soldered joints — what do such figures mean? The incredible ingenuity of man in the service of man — automatic telephony, the dial system, almost human in its operation, uncannily efficient buzzing, clicking, rat-a-tat-tat . . . .

The Post Office invites you to see the automatic dial system at work. Ring up your local telephone exchange for an appointment.

TELEPHONE

An advertisement of the Post Office Telephone Service

ABOVE: *The Post Office was proud of the rapid modernisation of the 1930s and was keen to advertise the benefits of automatic telephones. Today it is perhaps difficult to imagine the novelty of dial telephones.*

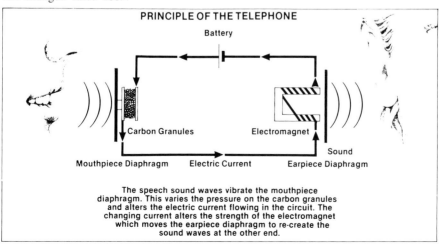

PRINCIPLE OF THE TELEPHONE

Battery

Carbon Granules   Electromagnet

Sound

Mouthpiece Diaphragm   Electric Current   Earpiece Diaphragm

The speech sound waves vibrate the mouthpiece diaphragm. This varies the pressure on the carbon granules and alters the electric current flowing in the circuit. The changing current alters the strength of the electromagnet which moves the earpiece diaphragm to re-create the sound waves at the other end.

The telephone came to Britain in 1878, just two years after its invention, when it was demonstrated before Queen Victoria. This 'butterstamp' telephone was used for both speaking and listening.

THE STORY OF THE TELEPHONE IN BRITAIN

The authorship of the telephone is disputed. In 1861 Reis had displayed a form of telephone in Germany. The first person to transmit recognisable speech through wires, however, was Alexander Graham Bell, who made this achievement in Boston, Massachusetts, in 1876. Born on 3rd March 1847 in Edinburgh, he attended university there and in London and did not emigrate until the age of twenty-three, when forced by declining health to seek cleaner air in America. Bell's profession was teaching the deaf and in his spare time he experimented with sending musical sounds by means of

telegraphy. In the process he also discovered a device which could transmit and receive speech.

People were not slow to see the potential of the new telephone and the following year, 1877, Bell sailed for Britain to promote his invention. In January 1878 he demonstrated the telephone to Queen Victoria at Osborne House, her home on the Isle of Wight. Commercial exploitation was quick to follow and the same year Bell established The Telephone Company Limited in London. A telephone exchange, the first in Britain, was opened at 36 Coleman Street, London.

Another American inventor, Edison, had patented a different pattern of telephone and he too opened a London telephone exchange. This was in 1879 at 11 Queen Victoria Street. The following year the two companies amalgamated, holding the patent rights to both inventors' systems, and used telephones taking the best ideas of both. The name of this undertaking was the United Telephone Company.

As the telephone began to realise a commercial significance the Post Office, which had the monopoly of transmitting telegrams, secured a High Court judgement that telephone calls were a kind of telegraphic message. The United Telephone Company — and other companies formed later — were allowed to continue, however, under a licence from the Post Office. From 1880 onwards the Post Office opened telephone exchanges of its own, while the private companies were amalgamating or becoming absorbed to form the National Telephone Company. In the main the National company exploited the larger towns, while the Post Office operated the trunk lines and telephones in the smaller towns and villages. Large towns like London were served by both organisations and the delays in making calls between one network and the other forced many customers to be subscribers of both systems. In old advertisements therefore, numbers for both National and Post Office systems may be quoted.

Trunk circuits linked London to Birmingham in 1890, Paris in 1891 and Glasgow, Belfast and Dublin in 1895. In 1899 an Act of Parliament was passed enabling municipalities to operate telephone systems, and Brighton, Glasgow, Kingston upon Hull, Portsmouth, Swansea and Tunbridge Wells all took out licences, though only Hull and Portsmouth lasted and were still in operation in 1912, when all other telephones (including Nation-

The Gower-Bell, one of the Post Office's first standard telephones. The receiver was inside the cabinet and two flexible tubes were held to the ears.

7

al's) were taken over by the Post Office. Portsmouth sold out to the Post Office in 1914 but an independent telephone system still operates in Hull.

Although the Strowger automatic telephone exchange dates from 1889 it was not easy to justify economically its immediate introduction in Britain. The first public exchange with dial telephones was opened at Epsom in 1912, and other exchanges of various designs followed. The first large exchange using a standardised Strowger system was opened in Leeds in 1918, and in the changed economic conditions after the First World War many more automatic exchanges followed.

Small rural communities were among the first to benefit from automation and now received twenty-four hour service from 'Unit Automatic Exchanges' or UAXs, several of which have been preserved. Technical development progressed rapidly between the wars: electronics were introduced, using valve amplifiers on trunk lines to boost the weak signals and also to combine many conversations on to a single cable in a technique known as carrier telephony. The first transatlantic telephone service, using radio, came in during 1927. In the same year the first 'director' exchange opened in London: the director technique allowed the Strowger automatic system to be used in large cities, using a three-letter exchange code in front of the number. Smart black telephones made of Bakelite, an early plastic, introduced a combined receiver-microphone handset and made the telephone something attractive to use. The heavy wooden and metal instruments, with their separate transmitters and receivers, were at last on the way out, and the Post Office was encouraging more people to be on the telephone.

During the Second World War the telephone played an important role: Britain developed the first underwater amplifier for submarine cable. Post Office research workers also devised Colossus, the world's first electronic computer, which was used to decode secret German messages. After the war improvements to the trunk network and systems to dial long-distance connections culminated in the introduction of Subscri-

For noisy locations the Post Office devised this 'horse collar' arrangement to enclose the Deckert-type transmitter. It did not last long, being considered unhygienic and faintly ridiculous.

8

LEFT: *By the 1880s the telephone had assumed a form which was to last for several decades. The only thing non-standard about this 'National' wall telephone is that the Blake transmitter is separate from the receiver.*

RIGHT: *Artistic design soon followed and by the beginning of the twentieth century some ornate patterns were in use. This is a standard Post Office wall telephone for the central battery system, Telephone number 1.*

ber Trunk Dialling (STD), which was inaugurated by Her Majesty the Queen in 1958. Five years later International Direct Dialling was introduced to Paris, and in 1971 New York was added to the growing list of overseas destinations.

Improvements continued with microwave radio links augmenting the cable network: the London Telecom Tower was opened in 1965, carrying not only telephone calls but also colour television signals for distribution to transmitters around Britain. In 1976 the last manual telephone exchange was closed and full STD became available in 1979. Other developments such as digital and optical fibre transmission and new designs of electronic and decorative telephones are scarcely history yet.

The 'skeleton' telephone. This classic design remained in production for thirty-six years after its introduction in 1895 and was used at Broadstairs into the 1950s and a decade longer on the railways. It represented a clever piece of industrial design as well as being artistic. The curved legs also form the magnets for the hand generator and the induction coil for the speech circuits is concealed inside the 'turret' below the handset cradle. This highly decorated example was supplied to the National Telephone Company, as the transfer shows.

TYPES OF TELEPHONE

Since the telephone was first invented many designs have been put into service, though nearly all fall into a few simple types or categories.

Telephones are normally wall or table types — in other words, they are either intended for mounting on the wall or free-standing to be used on a table or desk. Modern cordless and 'put it down anywhere' types are obvious exceptions, as are linemen's portable telephones and field telephones for military use. Up to the 1930s most telephones were wall types and desk telephones confined in the main to commercial subscribers. For this reason old desk sets are less common nowadays. Associated with the older

telephones were battery boxes, bellsets (or ringers) and hand generators: in wall instruments these were normally combined with the telephone, but for desk or table telephones they were in separate wooden cases. Often the bellset was fixed high up on a wall and survived many years longer than the telephone.

Telephones are also classed into automatic and non-automatic patterns, dependent on the type of exchange they were connected to. In some cases automatic, or at least convertible, telephones were provided on manual exchange lines. Dial telephones are not necessarily modern, though instruments used with the very earliest exchanges are now scarce. A special case is the intercommunication or intercom telephone, used in offices: these use separate wires instead of an exchange to 'buzz' the required instrument.

Telephones can also be categorised by their original use: public exchange, commercial (railways, factories, etcetera), domestic ('house telephones'), mining or military. This is because different patterns of instrument were manufactured for different classes of use. We are all familiar with telephones used on public exchanges, possibly not with other types. House telephones were simpler and more cheaply made than exchange telephones, and mining telephones had to be spark-proof — they were also used in gasworks and other places with explosive atmospheres. Telephones used in commercial installations — along railway lines or between power stations and substations, for instance — had to operate over long distances economically and with little maintenance. Specialised telephones were used with radiotelephone apparatus and on board ships, and all of these are found from time to time.

Telephones are energised by low-voltage direct-current electricity and consist of four basic components: the microphone (or transmitter), the receiver (or telephone), an alarm (normally a bell or buzzer) and some means of calling up 'the other end'. This last may be a dial to signal the required number to the exchange or it may be a press button or magneto generator to ring a bell. In the latter case the caller may be required to send a sequence of rings in a code, as when several users are connected on a party line.

As the power to energise the transmitter may be supplied from a battery of cells nearby or down the line from the exchange we distinguish between local battery (LB) and central (or common) battery (CB) instruments. The ringer or buzzer to receive calls may be designed to work on alternating current (AC) or direct current (DC); DC bells have a single gong whereas AC bells normally require two. Battery calling telephones are fitted with a press button to connect the battery to line, while for AC signall-

LEFT: *A 'National' table instrument for use on magneto exchanges. The picture is dated 1900 but the telephone would have been out of date then. It is also rather bulky for the average desk.*

RIGHT: *Another example of the skeleton: note the nickel-plated metalwork and the elaborate transfers on the japanned black legs. The Post Office, which designated this the Tele 16, had their instruments finished in plain black, with all non-painted parts oxidised, as this was considered more durable. (Collectors should beware of examples bearing both the number 16 and transfers: they are almost certainly not genuine.)*

ABOVE LEFT: *For all its attractive looks the skeleton telephone was not a success: the exposed parts tended to tarnish and could trap fingers. The next type, dating from around 1905, was this all-enclosed pattern, commonly called a 'corporation set' as many were supplied to the new municipal systems. This example, however, carries the emblem of the National Telephone Company (UK Bell system) and was their type NT13.*

ABOVE RIGHT: *This type of telephone was designated number 59 by the Post Office: the high number indicating it was a type taken over from the National Telephone Company. This is the payphone version with a coin slot at the top.*

BELOW: *A variant of the type NT13 telephone was supplied to the Post Office and known as their number 88 pattern. The wooden top was stained and varnished, while the steel side panels were printed with a realistic 'wood grain' finish.*

ing a hand generator or magneto is used. Magneto ringing can generate quite high voltages (up to 75 volts) and will operate over longer distances than battery ringing, though the cost of providing generators is higher.

Another category of old telephone is the restored or reproduction instrument. Large quantities of old Post Office candlestick and Scandinavian telephones were dressed up during the late 1960s for sale to unselective antique collectors, though the modifications destroyed their authenticity. Nowadays some reproductions are made of old telephones, for sale as ornaments or actual use, and there are also some which come under the refurbished or outright fake category.

ABOVE: *One of the types of telephone used on central battery signalling (CBS) exchanges: this bellset, photographed in 1906, has cow gongs giving a very distinctive and pleasant note.*

RIGHT: *Another CBS telephone, the type 26. This example from 1900 has been mounted on a battery box to turn it into a wall telephone.*

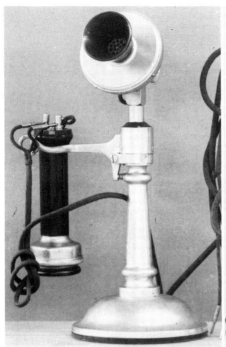

ABOVE LEFT: *Early candlestick telephones were extremely decorative and are now very rare. This example was made by the Western Electric Company (now STC) around 1907.*

ABOVE RIGHT: *The Post Office settled for a more prosaic design, finished in black. This number 2 type was used on manual exchanges from 1914 onwards.*

LEFT: *The original pattern had no provision for showing the subscriber's number: this was rectified by adding an engraved aluminium plate with a cut-out for a paper label behind it.*

14

HOW OFTEN DO PEOPLE FIND YOUR NUMBER ENGAGED?

Promotional advertising encouraged people to rent extra lines: it also demonstrated the new handset telephones at a time when most people used candlestick types.

TECHNICAL DESIGN AND PROGRESS

In this chapter some instruments which represent landmarks in the evolution to today's telephone are described. All of these are classic designs, though no judgement is intended on the artistic merit of their style and form. Where appropriate PO (Post Office) and NT (National Telephone Company) type numbers are shown.

THE CANDLESTICK TELEPHONE
(PO numbers 2, 4, 150)

This probably the first 'old telephone' to spring into people's minds. Other names are the pedestal telephone and the daffodil or tulip telephone (on account of the shape of the transmitter). Immortalised in films in Britain and the United States, it was never popular in most other countries, but with slight changes in

design it remained in common use in Britain from around 1900 until well into the 1950s.

The first British design was the number 2 type, which had no dial. The later number 150 pattern had space in the base for a dial (or a dummy used as a number label holder). The type number was normally stamped on the stem just below the transmitter.

Post Office instruments were all black but the National Telephone Company had nickel-plated versions. The original metal-cased 'solid back' transmitters had to be held upright in order to work properly, which accounted for the design of the telephone. Latterly these transmitters were changed for inset capsules in swivelling Bakelite housings. The telephone is not complete in itself and

ABOVE LEFT: *The standard form of Post Office dial telephone resembled the instruments used on manual exchanges. The number 8 pattern dial had a smaller centre label than today. This telephone dates from about 1924.*

ABOVE RIGHT: *The same number 150 telephone, but with the lettered dial used on 'director' exchanges in London. This telephone also has the number label on the transmitter.*

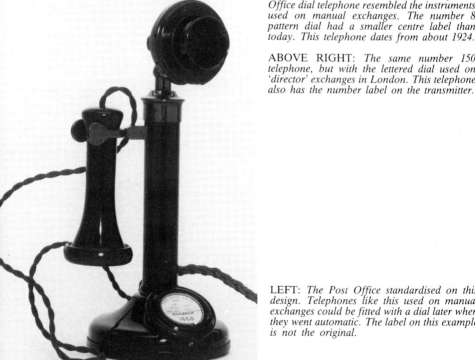

LEFT: *The Post Office standardised on this design. Telephones like this used on manual exchanges could be fitted with a dial later when they went automatic. The label on this example is not the original.*

requires a separate bellset, containing induction coil, capacitor and a ringer, to operate.

THE SKELETON TYPE *(PO number 16)*

This is another favourite design, which is highly prized now. It was manufactured from the late nineteenth century until the early 1930s. It formed the trade mark of the British L. M. Ericsson company for many years and most examples were made by Ericsson, in a number of countries. There is a bewildering number of variants of the skeleton design, and other manufacturers made copies, the most attractive being those by the Western Electric Company. Some people consider this to be the proper candlestick telephone, as the cradle is imagined to look like a candlestick or candelabrum.

The skeleton type is a magneto telephone, the curved legs forming the mag-nets of the generator; a few were converted to dial operation during the Second World War. Original Post Office instruments have a glossy black finish with oxidised (chemically bronzed or blackened) brass or aluminium transmitter and receiver housings. Instruments used on the National Telephone Company and private systems had nickel-plated components and black magnets. Filigree gold transfers were used to decorate the black parts and the total effect is impressive but when the Post Office took over these telephones it painted over the transfers.

TELE 88 AND THE CORPORATION TELEPHONES *(PO number 88, NT13)*

'Tele' is engineering jargon and a handy abbreviation for 'Post Office telephone type number', so a tele 88 is a number 88 type telephone. These magneto table instruments were the next de-

LEFT: *The rotary dial was not the only means of selecting a number automatically; the Canadian 'Lorimer' system used a different form of switch. An exchange of this type was installed by the Post Office at Hereford in 1914 but was not adopted elsewhere.*
RIGHT: *The wall telephone of the 1920s and 1930s was the 121. Note the polished wooden case and enamelled black dial.*

ABOVE: *A well used example of the number 121 discovered in Stony Stratford. The internal fittings, including large induction coil and Mansbridge condenser (capacitor) are shown on the right.*

BELOW: *The hand combination set (Post Office terminology for the handset telephone) was a great innovation when introduced in 1929 and was comfortable to use. It was also the first all-plastic telephone, produced originally in a mottled walnut brown finish, then in black, red, green and ivory.*

ABOVE: *Siemens Brothers christened this design the Neophone and GEC called their version the Gecophone — to the Post Office it was simply number 162. For busy people there was an autodial with a clockwork mechanism (right) to dial their frequently called numbers.*

BELOW: *The tele 162 could replace a candlestick telephone directly but at first still required the latter's wall-mounted bellset. This version includes a moulded bellset beneath the main phone. This one also has a black 'director' dial as used in London, Birmingham and other large cities. The dial label contains useful information.*

OPPOSITE, ABOVE: *A feature new to the tele 162 was the 'cheese tray' in the base. It slid out to reveal a celluloid holder for dialling instructions. The limited selection of codes gives a fascinating insight into the development of subscriber trunk dialling.*

RIGHT, ABOVE: *The first wall telephone with a handset was the number 221, rebuilt from a number 121 (note the plugged holes in the front). The case was painted black to match the handset.*

OPPOSITE, BELOW: *A cheese tray was also provided on telephone number 332, introduced in 1936. From the outset it was designed with a built-in bell and proved to be a very robust instrument. Early versions had a side cord entry and are now very rare.*

RIGHT, BELOW: *Moulded bakelite wall telephones were uncommon — there were probably sufficient wooden 221 types in the stores. This pattern was used in Australia and on London Transport's large private system.*

Another pattern, Post Office number 333, is seen here. The dial label, with unusual dialling codes, is from the internal Headquarters (now 01-432) exchange.

velopment on from the skeleton type. The generator was shrouded in a steel case to give it some protection and make manufacture simpler.

The whole instrument is very decorative, the case being printed with a woodgrain pattern (Post Office and National Telephone Company versions) or enamelled glossy black and transfer-printed with a coat of arms or badge (municipal and Ericsson proprietary versions). There are several variants of the internal circuitry, for example the NTC type NT13. Instruments used by the Post Office had notice frames with the caller's number and instructions on how to call up the exchange.

TELE 59 *(PO number 59, NT1)*

A classic design of wall telephone, familiar from old films, this was a magneto instrument designed by Ericsson, though other manufacturers had similar telephones. It was used by the Post Office, National Telephone Company and other organisations and many detail differences will be found but all contain the standard features of a writing desk and a large battery box to house two Leclanché cells. These telephones were popular with the NTC (their NT1 type), the corporations and electricity undertakings. There were also payphone versions. Transfers of the Ericsson emblem, the NTC bell or corporation arms may be found on the front of the battery box.

TELES 162 AND 232

The former General Post Office introduced these designs, which were the first central battery telephones with a 'hand combination', from 1929 onwards. Hand combinations (or handsets) were fine for local battery use but the type of transmitter used on central battery lines was not suitable for use in a handset — consequently the dated candlestick telephones were still being provided. These instruments were neither convenient nor comfortable to use for long conversations as they were too heavy. In view of all this the new handset telephone, moulded in Bakelite (then a modern material), was heralded as a major innovation.

The tele 162 was a direct replacement for the old number 150 and could use the same bellset on the wall. The 232 incorporated an anti-sidetone circuit, which reduced the pickup of background noise and was a significant improvement.

22

As a fashion item versions moulded in jade green, Chinese red and ivory were also introduced and these are highly prized today. (Previously the Post Office would repaint telephones to the customer's taste so long as the customer agreed to pay the cost of painting and of restoring the telephone to its original black.)

Another innovation was the 'cheeseboard', a sliding tray beneath the telephone which contained a dialling instruction card. Variants for payphone use exist as well as a neat wall version, which was not, however, adopted by the Post Office. The Post Office version required a separate bellset but instruments sold by Siemens Brothers (their Neophone) and the General Electric Company (the Gecophone) had a built-in ringer. A few examples are still in service.

TELE 332

Dating from the late 1930s and originally conceived in Sweden by Ericsson, this is an improved version of the earlier 232 instrument. It was a self-contained telephone, requiring no external bellset, and is still found in use. It, too, featured a 'cheeseboard' tray. It was normally a dial telephone, and many variants and coloured versions exist, as well as types with a magneto handle protruding from the 'dial' centre or the side of the case. It is frequently seen in Second World War films with either red or green handsets — the red telephones are priority and the green for scrambler use.

THE 700 SERIES TELEPHONE

The 700 family of designs is a modern classic, though already being supplanted by newer patterns. Inspired by the American 500 set and designed by the British Ericsson company (now incorporated in Plessey) it was introduced by the Post Office in 1959. From the beginning it was made available in a range of attractive colours, marking the end of black as the standard colour for a telephone. The normal colour for this telephone was two shades of grey, which set new trends in the colours of matching office equipment.

It was moulded in a new, easily cleaned plastic material and was much lighter than previous designs. Gone were the brown plaited rayon cords and a 'curly cord' was seen for the first time. A number ring surrounded the dial, which itself originally had no letters or numerals. The circuit incorporated a number of improvements including a more sensitive receiver and a plug-in current regulator to adjust sensitivity to the type of line. Many variants exist, including wallphones and unusual patterns of dial with spokes or dimples instead of the normal finger holes.

The 700 series telephone characterised the new look of the 1960s. Together with new styling this telephone introduced vastly improved transmission performance. This example of a number 706 was produced in clear plastic for display purposes.

23

For a long time railway signal cabins remained the last refuge of old telephones. This photograph of Luffenham Junction was taken in 1968. Many signal boxes have now disappeared and most of the telephones have been replaced.

USERS OF TELEPHONES

Not all old telephones to be seen nowadays were used in homes and offices, nor were all owned by the Post Office. The majority of those illustrated in this book are Post Office telephones, however.

The Post Office took the provision of telephones seriously and, unlike the other users of telephones, avoided all unnecessary decoration on them. It aimed for solid, reliable designs of instrument which tended to remain unchanged for long periods and to be distinctly plain and workmanlike. Every pattern of telephone was type-numbered and branded with a code indicating its year of manufacture and the maker. A typical code would be *No. 162 222/W33.* The first number is the pattern of telephone, in this case the first design of Bakelite table telephone. Even numbers are desk telephones and odd numbers denote wall instruments. The digits *222* are the mark number and *W33* is a code indicating the manufacturer — in this case the Standard Telephone Company (originally the

Western Electric Company) — and the year it was made, 1933. A list of manufacturer codes is given at the end of the book, and the type numbers of most old telephones can be identified from the books *Telephony* by Atkinson and *Telephony* by Herbert and Procter.

Whereas the Post Office designed most of its own telephones (or at least modified proprietary designs) the other users of telephones tended to buy 'off the shelf'. Instruments could be customised, and telephones supplied to the corporations and the National Telephone Company were invariably embellished with colourful transfers showing their name and emblem (a large bell for the NTC and the municipal arms for the corporations).

The next largest groups of users of telephones were the railways and other public utilities. The railways were fast to realise the improvement in operating efficiency made possible by telephones and it was not long before every station and most signal cabins were on the telephone (for many years the railways have had a private system rivalling the public network in size and complexity). Many of the railway telephone circuits were lengthy, connecting a large number of stations and signalboxes as well as being linked to exchanges at each end of the circuit. Ingenious devices were used to arrange selective ringing, for which battery (direct current) signalling was better suited. On some routes, however, 'bridging' circuits of magneto telephones were used and as these circuits might be 60 miles (96 km) or more long powerful magneto generators with four or five magnets were used.

Magneto telephones are very reliable and have also been installed in gasworks, waterworks and on electricity undertakings. Most of the old instruments have now been replaced but the system and fundamental circuitry of the telephones remains unchanged, except that a transistorised inverter device now converts battery voltage into alternating current and replaces the magneto generator.

Shops, offices, factories and hospitals are and were also large users of private telephone systems. Because the distances to be covered are usually short battery call telephones are generally used. Where a number of points or 'stations' need to communicate with each other an 'intercom' telephone system has been the usual choice since the beginning of the twentieth century. Numbered push buttons or a selector switch are used to select and call the desired station, and a multi-core cable is used to connect the instruments.

Above a dozen or so stations the complexity and cost of cabling become prohibitive and a small PAX (private automatic exchange) is installed instead. Many of these were installed between the

LEFT: *Not all telephones were used on public exchanges. This example was supplied by Western Electric to the London and North Western Railway Company, whose successors made good use of it until 1968. It had survived in an electricity sub-station, where its infrequent use had not necessitated its replacement. Power stations and gasworks are fruitful locations for forgotten old telephones.*
RIGHT: *This wooden magneto wall telephone also survived in use until 1968 — it was supplied to the London and North Western Railway in 1912. It was the LNWR's number 7 type and was made by the Peel Conner company of Coventry, a subsidiary of GEC.*

wars, and both exchange and telephones were usually of German manufacture because the British firms were engaged on larger public exchange work.

House telephones were very popular in the 1930s and earlier in the larger homes where servants were employed. Originally call bells were used to summon the staff but a telephone was a more satisfactory means of communication. Large country estates would have a telephone system entirely independent of the Post Office, linking various departments such as the stables, garage and farm agent. Purely domestic systems were invariably of the battery call type, sometimes reusing the old bell wiring and pushes. The more elaborate systems connecting the big house with outlying lodges and yards used 'low resistance' magneto bells and generators, on account of the distances involved.

House telephones are a specialised form of telephone used for domestic purposes in large houses. In many cases they used the wiring previously provided for the bell pushes which summoned servants. Designs were generally ornate, in true Victorian fashion.

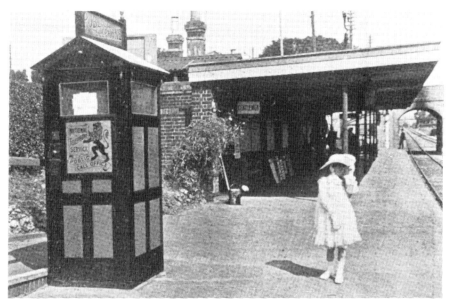

Looking rather like a sentry-box is this National Telephone Company payphone at Gosport Road station (now closed), near Portsmouth. Calls must have been untimed – note the penny-in-the-slot mechanism on the door, rather like a public toilet! Note also the men working on the railway telegraph wires in the background.

KIOSKS AND OTHER TELEPHONE APPARATUS

Apart from the old telephones themselves, there is much other interesting equipment, such as kiosks, switchboards switches and so on.

Britain's many public payphones owe their origin to a decision made in 1884, when the Postmaster General empowered the telephone companies to establish public call offices. At that time there were little more than thirteen thousand telephones in use, mainly by firms and well-to-do households, and the idea of a non-subscriber being able to make a telephone call for 2d was a novelty. Most of the early payphones were in shops, which discouraged some potential users, who felt obliged to buy something in the shop. Other telephones were inside post offices or railway stations, but by 1900 free-standing kiosks began to appear on the streets. Designs varied widely and about the only common feature was the 'Public telephone — You may telephone from here' sign. The National Telephone Company's signs had blue letters on white, while the Post Office version was in white on blue. A few of these signs are still to be seen.

Not all the early payphones had a coinbox built into them: some of the kiosks had a penny-in-the-slot mechanism on the door while others had an attendant to collect the fee. Many of the first kiosks were quite decorative — some were even thatched or made of rustic woodwork — but there was a need for a standard design which was easily recognisable as a telephone kiosk. In 1921 the first such design appeared, known simply as kiosk number 1. It was made of concrete with a red wooden door and was surmounted by a fearsome-looking spear. Though successful and long-lived (a few still survive), its design was rather plain and some metropolitan councils virtually refused to allow it on their streets. A

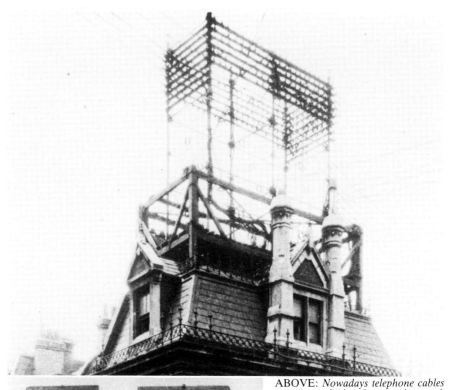

ABOVE: *Nowadays telephone cables in cities are laid underground or roof-top microwave links are used. In days gone by, however, the wires were taken across the rooftops to avoid digging up the roads. Enormous standards had to be erected on the roofs of telephone exchanges, and sometimes the accumulated weight of snow brought them crashing to the ground.*

LEFT: *For switching a telephone between an exchange line and an extension a variety of switches have been used. These are some, together with ringing keys for selective ringing.*

more attractive design was called for and to find this a competition was announced.

Kiosk number 2 was an all cast-iorn structure, designed by the noted architect Sir Giles Gilbert Scott. Its design and all-over bright red finish mark it as a classic. First introduced in London and provincial cities in 1927, it also is still to be seen today. A similar looking kiosk, made of concrete, was brought in in 1929 (kiosk number 3) but it did not weather as well as the iron version. Even more familiar than these designs is the 'Jubilee' kiosk (number 6), also designed by Gilbert Scott. From 1936 it became the first national standard design and is still the most widespread pattern of kiosk, despite postwar innovations.

Besides 'You may telephone from here' there are other patterns of public telephone signs to be seen in a few places. In country areas telegraph poles still carry small red enamel plates with *VR* or *GR* crests warning of dire penalties to those who damage the wires. Other items of telephone interest to be sought out include bellsets and extension switches.

Extension bells were made to the same high standards as the telephones and were normally of polished mahogany. Some carried transfers with the maker's name (such as Relay System) or had cow-bell shaped gongs to make a distinctive sound. Very often they had a secret

LEFT: The Post Office's first standard kiosk design appeared in 1921 and was made chiefly of concrete. This kiosk number 1 is waiting to be installed. Examples can still be seen in Bembridge (Isle of Wight), at the Oxford telephone museum and at the Crich tramway centre in Derbyshire.
RIGHT: A more elegant kiosk was the number 2, designed by Sir Giles Gilbert Scott, who won the contest to design a cast-iron kiosk. It incorporated many improvements: note the perforated crown ventilator. The press button was used in manual exchange areas for emergency calls.

LEFT: *Kiosk number 3 was the third standard design and was made of concrete, a material that turned out to be less durable than intended. Also designed by Sir Giles Gilbert Scott, it was originally intended for use in scenic areas and sites of special architectural importance, but in practice it turned up in many 'ordinary' locations. The concrete was painted in a natural colour and the window frames were red. This mid 1930s photograph shows an example complete with wood-case CB telephone and the small coinbox.*

RIGHT: *Kiosk number 4 of 1930 was a complete post office in miniature, combining telephone call office, letter box and stamp machines. Only fifty entered service and they were not a complete success: the coils of stamps became damp and turned into a solid roll, while the noise of the stamp machines disturbed phone users. A few still survive in use, in Warrington, Bewdley and elsewhere.*

lock, requiring a special kind of key to open them. The bells often survive in old houses, as do lightning arresters, which generally were on a porcelain base with an enamelled steel or hard rubber-composition case, fixed with a thumbscrew.

Other telephone artefacts which may be encountered are various patterns of switch, used to connect a telephone to a choice of lines. In this way a single instrument could be used to answer calls arriving on a number of lines: these were common on railway installations. The 'inter-through' switch (NT14) was common at one time in houses, shops and offices where the exchange was normally answered at one point and an enquiry might need to be made to someone else in the building. At times the line could be left switched through to the other telephone. These switches have three positions, normally marked 'Speak to exchange', 'Speak to extension' and 'Exchange through to extension'.

POST OFFICE MANUFACTURER CODES

These are to be found on telephones of Post Office origin and indicate the firm which made them. There are hundreds of codes but these are the most common.

AK: Peel Conner (later GEC).
C: General Electric Company (GEC).
E: British Ericsson Company (later Plessey).
FB: GPO Factory, Birmingham.
FH: GPO Factory, Holloway (London).
FW: GPO Factory, Wales (Cwmcarn).

The R suffix (e.g. FHR) indicated refurbished at FH.
H: Automatic Telephone & Electric (later Plessey).
I: Ibex Telephones.
PL: Plessey.
PX: Phoenix.
S: Siemens Brothers (later AEI).
TE: Telephone Manufacturing Company.
W: Western Electric (later STC).

MARKINGS INSIDE TELEPHONES

The terminals can be marked in a number of ways, which may be confusing when interpreting old circuit diagrams. The 'line' wires connecting telephones are taken to the terminals marked A and B, La and Lb, $L1$ and $L2$ or L and E. The battery connections for local battery telephones are marked C and Z, MC and MZ, or more obviously + and –. Z stands for zinc and C for carbon, for a dry battery has a carbon rod (the positive terminal) and an outer case of zinc (the negative terminal). The microphone (M) voltage is 3 volts: anything higher will soon burn out the transmitter.

Battery call phones may have terminals marked RC and RZ for the ringing voltage (normally 6 volts). Long-distance battery call telephones require a separate bell supply of 4.5 volts, across BC and BZ. Sometimes all positive poles are taken to a common connection marked C. E denotes the earth connection, which implies that the telephone incorporates a lightning arrester or is intended for party-line working in which the bell is connected between one line and earth. ER stands for extra receiver and two terminals marked EB are for connecting a series extension bell after the strap connecting the EB terminals has been removed.

FURTHER READING

Arden, Y. *Telephone Cards.* Shire, 1994.
Atkinson, J. *Telephony.* Pitman, 1948.
Goss, M. *Britain's Public Payphones.* British Telecom, 1984.
Johannessen, N. *Telephone Boxes.* Shire, second edition 1999.
Jolley, E. J. *Introduction to Telephony and Telegraphy.* Pitman, 1968.
Povey, P. *The Telephone and the Exchange.* Pitman, not dated.
Povey, P. J., and Earl, R. A. J. *Vintage Telephones of the World.* Institution of Electrical Engineers, 1988.
Smith, S. F. *Telephony and Telegraphy.* Oxford University Press, 1978.

The following titles are included for historical interest. Although out of print, they can be obtained through libraries and may be found in second-hand bookshops.

Herbert, T. *The Telephone System of the British Post Office.* Whittaker, 1904.
Herbert, T., and Procter, W. *Telephony.* Pitman, 1932.
Molloy, E. *House Telephones, Bells and Signalling Systems.* Newnes, 1940.
Poole, J. *The (Practical) Telephone Handbook.* Pitman, many editions.
Stevens, Captain E. *Field Telephones and Telegraphs.* Crosby Lockwood, 1917.

The Telecommunications Heritage Group was founded in 1987 for people interested in the history of telephones and telegraphs. The group arranges meetings and publishes a regular magazine. For more information write with a stamped addressed envelope to Telecommunications Heritage Group, PO Box 561, South Croydon, CR2 6YL.

PLACES TO VISIT

Many museums have one or two old telephones, even if these are only as an incidental exhibit, such as in Harding's Drapery Store at the Castle Museum, Eye of York, York (telephone 01904 613161), or on the preserved railways. However, there are several museum collections devoted to telecommunications and these are listed below together with some other museums that have good displays of old telephones: the list is not intended to be exhaustive. Opening arrangements may change so please check before making a long journey. Some of these museums are opened only by appointment and a telephone call will be necessary in these cases. There are also collections of old equipment in other places but these are not yet ready for viewing.

The Almonry Heritage Centre, Abbey Gate, Evesham, Worcestershire WR11 4BG. Telephone: 01386 446944. Excellent local museum with surprisingly large collection of old telephones. Website: www.evesham.uk.com

Amberley Museum, Amberley, Arundel, West Sussex BN18 9LT. Telephone: 01798 831370. Opposite Amberley station, easy road access. Comprehensive industrial archaeology museum, with a good section on telecommunications, including a restored rural telephone exchange. Website: www.amberleymuseum.co.uk

Avoncroft Museum of Historic Buildings, Stoke Heath, Bromsgrove, Worcestershire B60 4JR. Telephone: 01527 831886 or 831363. Buildings spanning seven centuries have been re-erected here, from windmills to prefabs. British Telecom has assisted by supplying examples of all its designs of telephone kiosk. Website: www.avoncroft.org.uk

Cabinet War Rooms, Clive Steps, King Charles Street, London SW1A 2AQ. Telephone: 020 7930 6961. Churchill's underground wartime headquarters, re-created to look as if it has been left as it was at the time of the Blitz. All telephone equipment on show. Website: www.iwm.org.uk

Design Museum, Butler's Wharf, Shad Thames, London SE1 2YD. Telephone: 020 7403 6933. A small number of design classic telephones are on show. Ericophon and other old GPO telephones for sale. Website: www.designmuseum.org

The Telephone Historical Centre, 10437 83rd Avenue, Edmonton, Alberta, T6E 4T5, Canada. Telephone: 001 780 433 1010.

Secret Wartime Tunnels, Dover Castle, Kent CT16 1HU. Telephone: 01304 211067. Tour of once secret wartime installations buried deep inside the cliffs includes tour of communications room, with large quantities of old switchboards, amplifiers and other equipment. Tours of the secret underground tunnels leave approximately every 15 minutes in summer and every 45 minutes in winter and take 50 minutes. The last tour starts at 17.00 in summer and at 15.00 in winter.

National Railway Museum, Leeman Road, York YO26 4XJ. Telephone: 01904 621261. Mainly trains but some telephone and telegraph exhibits also.

Royal Corps of Signals Museum, Blandford Camp, Dorset DT11 8RH. Telephone: 01258 482248. Signposted from the B3082 Blandford to Wimborne road. Contains a comprehensive display of military line and radio communications. Website: www.royalsignals.army.org.uk/museum

Royal Museum of Scotland, Chambers Street, Edinburgh EH1 1JF. Telephone: 0131 225 7534. Website: www.nms.ac.uk

Science Museum, Exhibition Road, South Kensington, London SW7 2DD. Telephone: 020 7942 4000. Telecommunications gallery with many interesting exhibits (plus many other items in store). Website: www.sciencemuseum.org.uk